Read All About It

Bill Ridgway

Cartoons by Roy Schofield

Edward Arnold

First published 1976
by Edward Arnold (Publishers) Ltd
25 Hill Street, London W1X 8LL

ISBN 0 7131 0037 0

The publisher wishes to thank the *Daily Mirror* and the *Staffordshire Evening Sentinel* for granting permission to reproduce the newspaper extracts in this book.

A list of Contents is on page 48.
Designed by DP Press Ltd.,
Sevenoaks and printed in Great
Britain by Unwin Brothers Ltd.,
The Gresham Press,
Old Woking, Surrey.

Read All About It

'Read all about it!' You have probably heard the newspaper seller's cry, as he sells his papers from the street corner. Perhaps you have a daily paper delivered to the place where you live. Or maybe your mother or father buys an evening paper on the way home from work.

In the early days of newspapers, only a few were printed. A well-known Sunday paper, which now sells over 6 000 000 copies every week, sold less than 13 000 in 1843. This was partly because many people could not read, and partly because many more could not afford to buy a paper. Today all this has changed, and several million national papers are sold every weekday in Britain.

Why do people still buy newspapers when they can get their news from television and radio? The answer to that isn't very clear, but here are some possible reasons: (i) You can read a paper at any time. You don't have to wait for the TV or radio news to begin; (ii) You can take a paper with you anywhere; (iii) You can look at a paper more than once to remind yourself of any facts you may have forgotten; (iv) Reading a paper in your own time gives you a chance to think about the news items and enjoy the articles.

There are two kinds of newspaper – the national or daily, which is available each morning nationwide, and the local, which deals mainly with news in the area where you live. In this book, you'll be looking at both kinds.

You will find articles taken from a well-known daily paper and from a local one – and some questions on each article. By doing the exercises you may find you begin to enjoy reading a newspaper. You will also learn what sort of items to expect in a newspaper. Remember, before you try any of the problems in the book, study the cuttings on the opposite pages very closely. In fact, 'Read all about it.'

Signs of the Zodiac

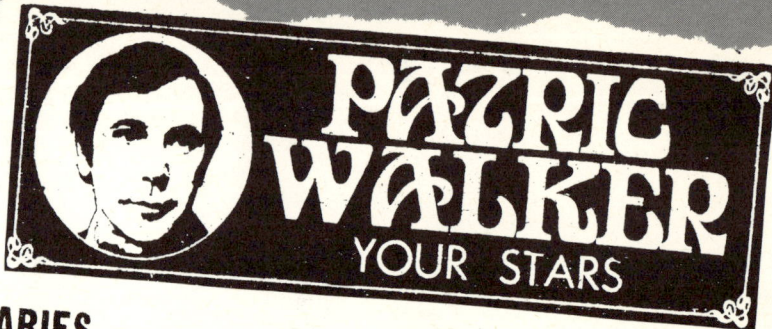

PATRIC WALKER
YOUR STARS

SAGITTARIUS (Nov. 22-Dec. 21):
Allow for delays and disruptions at work today and let others take over if you feel under par.

CAPRICORN (Dec. 22-Jan. 19):
Recent events have probably exhausted you emotionally so that you can no longer take an objective view of relationships. Not a day to question other people's motives.

AQUARIUS (Jan. 20-Feb. 19):
You may be trying too hard and creating problems for yourself both at home and at work. Try to be more optimistic.

PISCES (Feb. 20-March 20):
Everything related to communication, news and travel is rather unfavourably aspected today. Don't allow disappointments to influence your judgment of others.

ARIES (March 21-April 19):
Financially, this is an uncertain and difficult time. It will be hard to extract your dues or your rights in legal negotiations.

TAURUS (April 20-May 20):
The Moon in your birthsign today is bound to make you over-sensitive. Make sure you don't injure relationships by being too demanding.

GEMINI (May 21-June 20):
You won't be at your best mentally or physically today. Don't place too much value on what is said or intimated.

CANCER (June 21-July 22):
Friendships and emotional attachments are emphasised today. Advise others without being too dogmatic.

LEO (July 23-Aug. 22):
Unfavourable aspects today may create some kind of a dilemma at home and at work. But don't abandon your plans.

VIRGO (Aug. 23-Sept. 22):
You may know what needs to be said today, but choose the right moment. If you don't, loved ones and associates will take offence.

LIBRA (Sept. 23-Oct. 22):
You can't evade issues today, particularly financial ones. At the same time, there is no need to argue over trivialities.

SCORPIO (Oct. 23-Nov. 21):
Mercury and Mars in your birthsign may fire you with imagination and determination. But remember that you have obligations to others which you must fulfil today.

Signs of the Zodiac

3 Find out how the signs of the Zodiac first came about.

4 There is a drawing for each sign of the Zodiac. See if you can find these drawings, and copy a few of them out. Put the name of the sign under each drawing.

A 1 Sagittarius and Capricorn are both signs of the Zodiac. Make a list of the other ten signs.

2 What is the sign for people whose birthdays come between June 21st and July 22nd?

3 John was born under Leo. His birthday must have been between which two dates?

4 Janet was born on October 27th. What advice is given to her?

5 If you find yourself 'trying too hard and creating problems for yourself both at home and at work', you were probably born under which sign?

6 Susan 'can't evade issues today, particularly financial ones'. Between which two dates is her birthday?

7 (a) Which sign mentions the Moon?
   (b) Which sign mentions two planets?

8 Write down the date of a friend's birthday, the sign he or she was born under, and what advice is given.

9 Write down *your* sign of the Zodiac.

B 1 Do you believe in fortune telling? Give reasons for your answer.

2 Find out the meanings of these words:
   predict   astrology.

'It says I'm going to meet a dark stranger who'll sweep me off my feet.'

5

New petrol price shock

Energy supremo's New Year message

SLOW DOWN AND COOL OFF !

MAKE the most of this Christmas. The war on fuel-wasting begins in earnest in the New Year.

That was the chilly message from Energy Secretary Eric Varley last night as he spelled out his measures to save Britain's fuel bill.

For the next few years, life will be not so hot indoors, not so bright in the high streets, and not so fast on the roads.

Headlines

A 1 Write down the five main words of the headline.

2 Write down any **white** lettering you see in the headline.

3 Write down the four words that **introduce** the headline.

4 How many sizes of print make up the complete headline?

5 Find out what these words mean:

   supremo   **in earnest.**

6 How many sizes of print are there in the whole clip?

7 Write down the two sentences that make most sense to you:

   Headlines are big because they deal with the most important news.

   Headlines are big because all headlines are big. People buy the newspaper with the biggest headlines.

   Headlines are big so that they will attract your attention.

8 Apart from big letters, what else makes these headlines stand out?

9 Write down the sentence which you think makes most sense:

   The first sentences are the ones which introduce the article and they are in thick black letters to make them stand out.

   The first sentences are in thick letters to show they are not important.

   The first sentences are in thick black letters because the newspaper men could not find the right printing machine.

10 Write down the sentence printed in the smallest letters.

B 1 Do you think the headline is from **A** the front page, **B** a middle page, or **C** the back page? Write down **A, B** or **C.**

2 Compare a day's headlines from your local paper with those of a daily paper. What differences can you find?

3 Compare a day's headlines in several different daily papers. Write down the different headlines and put the name of each paper by its headline. Tick the headlines which deal with the same piece of news.

Advertisements

First advertisement

A 1 What is the first thing you notice when you see the advertisement?

2 What is being advertised? (two words)

3 There are two illustrations:

The first shows a man who is ...

The second shows three ...

Copy out and complete the sentences.

4 Copy out these sentences and fill in the blanks:

The ingredients of the powders and tablets are said to relieve _____ , _____ and pains.

Beecham's powders come in either _____ , _____ or _____ form.

5 What is a **special formula**?

6 Divide the advertisement into two parts. What are the three main words in the top part? What are the six main words in the bottom part?

Second advertisement

7 Write down all the words that stand out in the advertisement.

8 Describe the picture. What sort of expression is on the boy's face?

9 You can enter the RAF at 15, 16 or 18 years of age. Which?

10 Copy out the coupon and fill it in.

11 How do you find out about life in the RAF? Where do you call for an 'informal chat'?

12 What is HA7 4PZ? What is 'the UK'?

13 Write down the 'odd one out' in these sentences:

The two advertisements make use of different type sizes.

The two advertisements make use of photos and writing.

The two advertisements use photos of people to help sell the product.

The two advertisements make use of coloured illustrations.

B 1 Design an advertisement of your own to sell an imaginary product. Look at other advertisements to get some ideas.

2 Look at some coloured advertisements for cars or kitchen units. Are cars or kitchens in real life the same as those in the advertisements, or are they different? If they are different, how are they different?

TV and Radio

BBC-1

9.30—SCHOOLS: Economics of the Real World; 10.0 Look and Read; 10.23 Ffenestri. .10.45 You and Me. 11.0 Schools: Scene; 11.30 A Job Worth Doing? 12.0 Engineering Craft Studies. 12.25 Pobol y Cym. (Not Wales, Ulster or Scotland.) 12.55 News.

1.0—PEBBLE MILL. 1.45 Mary, Mungo and Midge. 2.2 Schools: Tout Compris; 2.35 Twentieth-Century Focus. 2.55 Top Score: Musical Quiz.

3.25—ASPEL AND COMPANY. 3.58 News. 4.0 Play School. 4.25 Pixie and Dixie. 4.30 Jackanory, with Geoffrey Bayldon. 4.45 Speed Buggy.

5.10—CHILDREN OF DESTINY: The Farmer's Son. 5.35 The Clangers. 5.45 News. 6.0 Nationwide; Regional News Magazine. 7.0 Wonderful World Of Disney.

7.45—NO STRINGS: Rita Tushingham and Keith Barron in Look Before You Eat. 8.15 Farewell Gang Show, featuring the Scouts and Guides. 9.0 News. 9.25 The Detectives: Harry O. David Janssen in Mortal Sin.

10.15—INTRODUCING DIANE SOLOMON: Music and song, featuring a new personality. (Ulster; Austin Gaffney Sings). 10.45 Face Your Image: Lord Longford. 11.25 News. 11.33 Beachhead (film, 1954). 1.8 Weather.

BBC-2

11.0—PLAY SCHOOL. 1.50 Racing from Cheltenham (2.5, 2.40, 3.10, 3.40 races). 6.40 Poets on Poetry: Seamus Heaney. 7.30 Newsday with Robin Day.

7.45—WILDERNESS: The Himalayas. 8.15 The Money Programme: Healey in the High Street. 9.0 M*A*S*H: Alan Alda, Wayne Rogers in Henry In Love.

9.25—PARADISE RESTORED, with John Neville, Polly James, Anne Stallybrass. 10.50 In Vision: Television in America. 11.20 News Extra. 11.50 Julian Glover reads from Samson Agonistes.

MIDLANDS

9.30 Schools. 12.0 Pipkins. 12.15 Alister in Songland. 12.30 Kreskin. 1.0 First Report. 1.20 Cartoon. 1.30 Crown Court. 2.0 General Hospital. 2.30 Racing from Doncaster. 3.55 Good Afternoon. 4.20 The Jensen Code. 4.50 Magpie. 5.20 Elephant Boy. 5.50 News. 6.0 ATV Today. 6.35 Crossroads. 7.0 The Top Secret Life of Edgar Briggs. 7.30 Billy Liar. 8.0 Hawaii Five-O. 9.0 Intimate Strangers. 10.0 News at Ten. 10.30 Creature From The Black Lagoon (film, 1954). 12.0 Father Pascal.

RADIO 1 (247 metres): 5.0 News; Weather. 5.2 Simon Bates. 7.0 Paul Burnett. 9.0 Tony Blackburn. 12.0 Johnnie Walker. 2.0 David Hamilton. 5.0 Rosko. 7.0 As Radio 2. 10.0 Rockspeak. 12.0 As Radio 2.

RADIO 2 (1,500 metres): 5.0 News; Weather. 5.2 Simon Bates. 7.2 Terry Wogan. 9.2 Pete Murray. 11.30 Jimmy Young. 1.45 Ricochet. 2.2 Tony Brandon. 4.15 Waggoners' Walk NW. 4.30 Joe Henderson. 6.2 Sam Costa. 6.45 Sports Desk. 7.2 Punch Line. 7.30 Sing Something Simple. 8.2 Frank Chacksfield. 9.2 Friday Night is Music Night. 10.2 John Dunn. 12.0 News. 12.5 Night Ride. 2.0 News; Weather.

RADIO 3 (464 metres): 7.0 News; Weather. 7.5 Overture. 8.0 News; Weather. 8.5 Morning Concert. 9.0 News; Weather. 9.5 This Week's Composer. 9.55 Sing We at Pleasure. 10.25 Music from The Hunza. 10.55 Piano Recital. 12.20 Midday

TV and Radio

A 1 Which are the three TV channels shown here that you can switch to?
2 Write down the names of the three radio stations shown.
3 Copy down and complete this table:

Programme	Channel	Time
Nationwide	BBC 1	6.00 pm
Newsday		
Elephant Boy		
Beachhead		

4 What programme would I find on BBC 1 at 10.15 pm?
   What would I find on BBC 2 at 9.00 pm?
   What would I find on Midlands at 2.30 pm?
5 Which radio station would I switch to for pop music?
   Which for light music? And which for serious music?
6 Are there any disc-jockeys on Radio 3? (yes or no)
7 I am interested in the best way of saving my money.
   Which BBC TV programme may be able to help me?
8 How long does M * A * S * H (BBC 2, 9.00 pm) last for?
9 How many times is there News on BBC 1?
   How many times on BBC 2?

B 1 Why do you think television programmes are printed in bigger type than radio programmes?
2 Find out from your science teacher what '247 metres', '1500 metres' and '464 metres' mean.
3 Compare ITV programmes with those of BBC 1 and BBC 2 in any one week. Find out which channel has the most drama, which the most comedy, news, music, etc. Your teacher will help you.
4 Find out which are the most popular TV programmes for each member of your class. Make a chart showing the top ten programmes. Discuss the chart with your teacher.

OH, SEW TRENDY

A STITCH in time can save you money—and put you among the trendies. Like this Butterick paper pattern of a fashionable calf-length skirt.

It is No. 3929 and costs 50p. The skirt above took 2¾ yards of 54-inch pure wool. We made it in one of the best prints and fabrics money can buy, at £4·92 a yard. Both print and pattern are available by mail order from Liberty, Regent Street, London, W.1—but of course you could make it out of cheaper material.

Our jumper is made of Shetland wool in various colours at £4, also at Liberty.

Fashion: LESLEY EBBETTS
Picture: DOREEN SPOONER

Fashion

A 1 Describe the girl in the picture.

2 What does **sew** mean? Where does the word come in the article? What word would you expect to find instead?

3 What does **trendy** mean?

4 Find the following numbers and say how each one comes into the article:

    3929   50p $2\frac{3}{4}$ yds   54 in.
    £4.92   £4

5 Is the skirt thigh length, knee length or calf length? Is the printed fabric good, average or poor? Write down another word for **fabric.**

6 What are a) Liberty, and b) Butterick, do you think?

7 Write down the address you could send to for the material and pattern.

8 How does the word **Shetland** come into the article? What does it mean?

9 Are the model's boots mentioned in the article? (yes or no)

B 1 Write down four colours you think you could buy the jumper in.

2 What is the meaning of the word **available**?

3 Design an outfit for a man or a woman to wear at a dance. Write a few lines describing the outfit you've drawn.

4 When you start work, some of the money you earn will be spent on clothes. Say you spent £150 on clothes in the first year. Make out a chart showing what you would buy and how much you would pay for each item. (This includes footwear.) Mind you don't overspend.

'That's what I like about Sue. She always dresses in style!'

Invasion scare for Doc !

Shelbourne 1, Man Utd 1

By TOM KEOGH

MANCHESTER United ran the gauntlet of bottle-throwing fans and an invasion of the pitch during this FRIENDLY in Dublin last night.

Tommy Docherty's men had to dash to the safety of the dressing room when a horde of youngsters charged on to the playing area early the second half.

They stayed there for 12 minutes while police ejected the trouble-makers and moved into position on the terraces from which bottles, nails and other metallic objects had been thrown.

I understand Docherty only agreed to allow his high-priced stars back into the game after receiving guarantees for their safety.

Later the Doc refused to be drawn by the ugly episode. All he would say at the team's hotel was: "I don't want to talk about it. I'm not bothered."

But the Second Division leaders must be asking themselves a lot of questions after the Irish part-timers. from whom they signed goalkeeper Paddy Roche 18 months ago, almost pipped them on the post.

Shelbourne refused to treat this game as just a bonus for the R o c h e signing. They got stuck in from the start and after 13 minutes Fran Swan rocketed the ball home.

Four minutes later Doc sent on Mick Martin and Willie Morgan in place of Brian Greenhoff and Stuart Pearson. who had been involved in several brushes.

And before half-time Jim McCalliog was helped off with an injured knee. after a hefty tackle by Swan.

When play re-started after the 12-minute hold up United, desperate to retrieve the situation. poured everything into attack.

But they had to wait until the 88th minute before Dubliner Gerry Daly slotted home a face-saving equaliser.

Sport

A 1 Are the following true or false?

The match took place in Dublin.

Tommy Docherty's men stayed where they were when a horde of youngsters charged on to the playing area.

The youngsters charged on to the pitch in the first half.

They stayed for twelve minutes.

Doc said, 'I want to talk about it.'

2 Answer **yes** or **no** to the following:

Did the Irish part-timers almost beat Manchester United?

Was Mick Martin sent on in place of Brian Greenhoff?

Was the face-saver slotted home by Dublin?

3 What do these phrases mean?

rocketed the ball home   **an equalizer**

pipped on the post   **face saving**

got stuck in

4 Who had an injured knee? Who was United's goal-keeper?

5 What do these words mean?

horde   **metallic**   **episode**   **bonus**

6 Who was the manager of Manchester United when this article was published?

B 1 Look in your local or a national newspaper for an account of any game you have seen on the field. Decide whether the article is a true account of the match or not.

2 Write an account of a match you have seen, or watched on TV.

'Fancy dribbler, that no. 10.'

15

LOAD OF BULL IN FLO'S BEDROOM

By CLIVE CRICKMER

BERTIE the bullock decided to sample a few home comforts yesterday. He leapt a fence, crossed a busy main road and trotted briskly a quarter of a mile to Mrs. Florence Waters's council house.

Then he pushed open the back door, marched through the kitchen and inspected the living room before deciding bed was the place for him.

He clambered up a twisting flight of fourteen stairs—his flanks rubbing against the walls of the stairway—before going into the back room, where he flopped across the bed.

Joking

And there he lay while Mrs. Waters's children Jane, seven, and Jacqueline, two, ran to tell their Mum of the intruder.

Mrs. Waters, 24, who had popped out to her parents' home nearby, thought at first that the children were joking.

And policemen who answered a 999 call to the house in Woodhorn Crescent, Newbiggin, Northumberland, were also sceptical.

But it was no cock-and-bullock story so far as 6½cwt. Bertie was concerned.

Several attempts to dislodge him failed before his owner, general dealer Mr. Bill Graham, arrived on the scene.

Mr. Graham and his son managed to put a rope around Bertie's neck and drag him out.

Animals

A 1 Copy out these sentences and fill in the missing
words from the article. Put one word on each line:
   Bertie leapt a_____, crossed a____ ____ _____,
   and trotted briskly to Mrs Florence Waters's
   council house.
   He ____ through the kitchen and_____the
   ____ ____.
   He___ ___ ___ twisting____ ____ ____stairs.

2 Here are some words from the clip. Fill in the
   missing letters, putting one letter on each dash.
   Copy out the whole word.

   J _ _ _ _uel_ _ _ _(a name)
   N _ _ _ _ u _ b _ _ _ _ _ _ _(a county)
   _ _ _ _eral _ _ _ _ _ _er (a job)

3 What do these words mean?
   **flanks   intruder   dislodge
   sceptical**

4 Name two children in the story.
   Name the bullock's owner.
   What is Mrs Waters's first name?

5 How does 999 come into the story? How does 6½ cwt
   come into the story?

6 What do you think 'It was no cock-and-bullock
   story' means?

B 1 Find other animal stories in the papers and read
them. Which animal is written about most often?

2 See if you can find out which newspaper prints
animal stories most often. Cut out all the animal
stories you can find and see if you can divide them
into funny stories and serious ones.

3 Write a story about the bullock in the article as
though he had just walked into *your* home.

'What d'you mean, you're looking for worms?'

TIFF—THEN JENNY HITS THE ROOF

By MIRROR REPORTER

TEENAGE wife Jenny McDonnall really hit the roof when she had a row with her husband yesterday.

She grabbed a ladder from the garage and climbed up there.

And for more than three hours, 19-year-old blonde Jenny stayed on the roof of their home in Elmers End Road, Anerley, South London.

Shock

Her husband Patrick, 21, spent an hour pondering what to do before he called the fire brigade—and it took another two hours before Jenny was coaxed down.

But Patrick, a British Rail labourer, was in for another shock. Instead of a reconciliation pretty Jenny packed her bags and went home to Mum.

And Patrick doesn't know where Jenny's family is living at present.

"We've been married a couple of years and had rows before, but this one has been the worst," he said. "I only hope she'll be back soon."

Hungarian-born Jenny came to Britain as a child refugee after the 1956 uprising.

Her parents later emigrated from England to Australia, but recently came back.

"The last I heard they hadn't found anywhere permanent to live. That's why I don't know where to start looking for Jenny," said Patrick.

18

Bits and Pieces

A 1 What is a **tiff?**

2 If someone **hits the roof,** he is a) angry, b) smashing the tiles, c) putting up a television aerial. Which one?

3 Copy out and complete these sentences:
Jenny McDonnall hit the roof when . . .
Jenny stayed on the roof for more than . . .
Patrick called the . . .

4 Who grabbed a ladder from the garage?
Who was a British Rail labourer?
Who had been married for a couple of years?

5 Write down *all* the words that Jenny's husband says in the article.

6 Name the three countries mentioned in the article.

7 Think of a word that means the opposite of permanent.
What does **emigrated** mean?
What is a **reconciliation**?

8 What does the article tell you about a) the Fire Brigade; b) Jenny's parents?

9 Count how many paragraphs the article covers.

B 1 Find out what **verbs** are. Here are four words from the article, with their letters jumbled. See if you can sort them out. *Each word is a verb.*

deringpon   **xcoaed**   **oufnd**
klonige

2 What is a **refugee**?

3 Find out as much as you can about the Hungarian uprising of 1956.

'Of course it's a pair of briefs. What else do you expect to find in a brief-case?'

NEW WAR FEARS IN ISRAEL

Sunday Mirror Political Editor

FEARS that a new war between Israel and the Arabs may break out soon led to urgent "hot line" talks between America and Russia yesterday.

Large formations of Israeli troops and tanks have been reported moving towards the Syrian border in the Golan Heights.

The mandate for United Nations' peace-keeping forces along the border runs out on November 29.

Unless it is renewed by then the blue-helmeted troops will move out.

Some diplomats in New York see the Israeli pressure as a move to get the UN mandate extended.

But Israelis are determined not to be caught napping as they were in last October's clash.

And they are worried by reports that 20 Russian ships are unloading arms in the Syrian port of Latakia.

A new Middle East war could lead to a new disruption of oil supplies.

American and Russian leaders are believed to be trying to ease the tension.

In Tel Aviv Defence Minister Shimon Peres said Israel had mounted a precautionary alert because of "doubts about Syrian intentions."

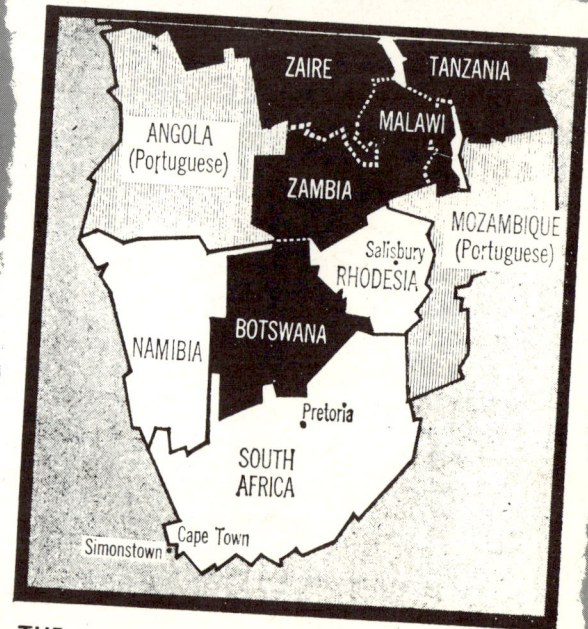

THE new situation confronting Rhodesian Premier Ian Smith. Almost surrounded by black states, he will now have an independent Mozambique as a neighbour. Map by TERRY DICKIE.

20

Foreign News

New War Fears in Israel

A 1 What is a **mandate**? Ask your teacher to help you.

2 Write down the correct sentence:

It is feared that a war may break out between America and Russia.

It is feared that a war may break out between Israel and the Arabs.

It is feared that a war may break out between the United Nations.

3 Answer **true, not true,** or **don't know,** after reading the following:

The mandate for UN peacekeeping forces runs out on November 29th.

The president of the United States was in Israel at the time.

4 What must be renewed if the UN forces are to stay along the border?

5 Complete and copy out the sentences:

The Israeli armies may be moving to try to force the UN to extend their . . .

The Israeli armies may be moving because they are worried by . . .

6 Who is the Israeli Defence Minister named in this article?

7 Find out what these phrases mean:

large formation of troops

caught napping   **precautionary alert**

hot line

Map of Africa

8 Make one list of the African states shown in white, and another of those shown in black.

9 What do the black and white areas on the map stand for?

B 1 See if you can discover the names of the leaders of the states shown on the map. Write the leader's name against his state.

2 Read anything you can find in the papers about the Arabs and Israelis.

3 Find out all you can about **anti-semitism.**

£20 CLUE TO KILLER

By CLIVE CRICKMER

SUB - POSTMASTER Edwin Waterson yesterday gave the slip to a gunman who may be a triple killer—and who stole only £20.

Mr. Waterson, a 60-year-old former Army major, made the daring dash to freedom as he was being forced at gun-point to open his safe.

It followed the murders last year of three sub-postmasters — David Skepper at Harrogate, Derek Astin at Accrington, and Sydney Grayland at Birmingham.

Mr Waterson dived through a back door which the intruder had opened with a jemmy, and escaped over an eight-foot wall to raise the alarm.

The gunman fled from the post office in Lothian Terrace, Washington, Co. Durham, with only £20 in loose cash.

Last night Northumbria police believed he may be the man with a £25,000 price on his head after the killing of the three sub-post-masters.

Like the killer, the gunman was dressed in dark clothes and was masked.

He was again described as being fair-haired and in his early twenties.

Detective Chief Inspector Tom Garside, in charge of the manhunt, said: "We cannot ignore the possibility it is the same man."

The £25,000 reward for the killer was put up by the Post Office and the National Federation of Sub-postmasters.

Crime

A 1 Copy the sentences and fill in the blanks:

Mr Waterson's first name is _____ .

Mr Waterson is _____ years of age.

Mr Waterson used to be an _____ .

2 How did Mr Waterson escape?

3 Where was Mr Waterson's post office?

4 Describe the gunman.

5 Who is still willing to put up £25 000 and for what?

6 What do these words and phrases mean?

gave the slip to   **raise the alarm**

forced at gun point   **manhunt**

intruder   **jemmy**

B 1 Write a short story as if you were the sub-postmaster, telling what happened when the gunman broke into your post office, and how you escaped.

2 If you were in charge of law and order in this country, what punishment would you give for these crimes:

murder of a young child

an armed bank raid in which the thieves carried guns

a bank raid where the thieves carried coshes

rape?

'C'mon Dave, pass the wrench.'

23

Wild bird massacre starts big storm

NEARLY 200,000 blackbirds have been slaughtered amid a storm of protest by animal-lovers.

Huge heaps of the dead birds were discovered yesterday at Paducah, Kentucky, after a plane sprayed their roosting area with detergent.

The detergent damaged the bird's feathers, causing them to freeze to death.

Officials there ordered the spraying because, they say, the birds are a health hazard.

Doctors claim that their droppings cause a disease that attacks the respiratory system.

The birds had ignored all attempts to frighten them off with loud noises.

Despite protests by wildlife groups, the killing began after the U.S. Army got court permission last week to take similar action against another 12 million blackbirds on military camps and bases in the South.

From MARK DOWDNEY
In New York

The Army is still checking with scientists about the safety of mass spraying.

Awful

But Paducah went ahead on its own and dropped 1,400 gallons of the special detergent on Saturday night

"It was awful," said one wildlife observer. "They were dropping out of the trees like rainfall. It was a pitiful sight."

The Environment

A 1 a) How many birds have been slaughtered?
  b) Where were they slaughtered?
  c) Who was slaughtering them?
  d) Why were they slaughtered?
 2 a) How does the figure 200 000 come into the story?
  b) How does the figure 12 million come into the story?
 3 Choose the right meaning from the words in brackets and copy the sentences down:
  Slaughtered means _____ (maimed, killed, poisoned, sprayed).
  A detergent is _____ (a cleaner, a poisoner, an acid).
  Pitiful means _____ (worthy of pity, merciless, happy).
  Ignore means _____ (pay attention to, take no notice of, listen to).
 4 What phrases or groups of words from the article mean:
  a) a great deal of objection
  b) a danger to health
  c) the part of the body that deals with breathing?
 5 How did people try to frighten the birds off before using a spray?

B 1 Find a picture of a blackbird. Draw it. Find out as much as you can about the way a blackbird lives.
 2 Do you think it is cruel to kill thousands of birds as they were killed in the article? Was it necessary, do you think, for the birds to be killed in that way?
 3 Is it important to protect our wildlife, do you think? Say why. Make a list of ten wild birds you know and six wild animals.

'They won't get *us*!'

Situations Vacant

APPRENTICE required to train as Ladies Hairdresser. — Tel. Blythe Bridge 5978. 285

ARE you looking for extra cash for Christmas? Would £20 a week help? If you are of smart appearance, with vitality and personality, you could be the person we are looking for. — For interview telephone local Hanley office. S.O.T. 264254. m to f 290

ART Dealers require Junior to train in framing and restoration of art-works. We require a person with the natural desire to endeavour to achieve a perfect job. This position could lead to being departmental head on a profit sharing basis for the right person. — Tel. 84981. 284

AUDIO Typist reqd. for work in the Secretarial Services Dept. Preference will be given to applicants aged 16-18, who possess basic typing skills, training will be given. — Apply to: The Personnel Officer, Creda Electric Ltd., Blythe Bridge, S.O.T. Tel. Blythe Bridge 2281. 285

AUTO Electrician required. — Apply: Smithsons, Longton. Phone 35123. th f m 286

BAR Staff required, good wages. — The Swan, Newcastle-rd., Trent Vale. 44150. 284

BAR Staff wanted, part-time. — Apply: Manager, Trentham Hotel, 657316 285

BAR Staff required, evenings. — Apply: Noahs Ark, Hartshill, Ring 619478. f m t 287

BAR Staff wanted, part-time. — Apply: Steward, Norton Central Workingmen's Club. Phone. 534780. 285

BAR Staff required, also Cleaner. — John O Gaunt, Newcastle. Tel. 617634. 285

BAR Staff required, evenings and Sunday lunch. — Apply: Potters Wheel, Porthill 562471. 286

BAR Staff required, part-time, top rates paid. — Apply: Steward, Birches Head Gardeners' Club, Oak-st., Birches Head. Tel. 24998. 285

BAR Staff required. — Duke of Wellington, Lichfield-st., 25518. 284

BAR Staff required, part-time or full. — Apply: Steward, Smallthorne Victory Club, 300, Hanley-rd., 285

BAR Staff, male and female required for evening work, experience not essential, 50p per hour. — Apply: Windmill Inn, Meir Heath, Tel. Blythe Bridge 4759. 284

BAR Staff required. — Lord John Russell Hotel, Trentham-rd., Dresden 33106. 285

BARMAIDS required, lunch times. — Lord John Russell, Hanley. Phone 261578. 284

BARMAIDS required, lunches only. — Please phone Berni Tavern 622217. 286

BARMAID reqd., to star in the Footlights Bar with full supporting cast, of local businessmen and hotel guests, this would suit a young lady who has a bright personality and some bar experience, a 5-day 40-hour week is offered and the position is available now, with excellent rates of pay. — Please phone the Personnel Manager, at the North Stafford Hotel to arrange an interview, S.O.T. 48501. m w f 284

BARMAID 4 lunchtimes, top wages for suitable applicant. — Apply: Manager, Roman Candle, Hanley. x 284

BARMAID wanted. — Apply: Roebuck, Leek-rd., Stoke. Tel. 48744. 285

BARMAIDS required, part-time no previous experience required. — The Talbot Inn, Grange-rd., Biddulph, Tel. 512608. 285

BARMAIDS required, evenings or lunch. — Apply: Duke of York, Newcastle 615975. 284

BLUE Star Garages Ltd., require Forecourt Sales Staff, male or female, shift work, transport provided. — Apply: Keele Park 241. m to f 286

BONERS required. Top rates of pay for experienced men. — Apply: Mr. Evans, Towers of Stafford, 57, Gaol-road. Stafford. Tel. Stafford 51244. 285

CLEANERS, male, required, Hanley area, approx. 2 hours per evening. — Apply: Workforce, Town-rd., Hanley. Tel. 263032. 286

CLEANER required, 6 mornings per week, good rates of pay. — Apply: Sutherland Arms Newcastle 617830. 284

CLEANERS required in Longton. — Please ring S.O.T. 39286. 286

CLEANERS required in Etruria. — Please ring S.O.T. 39286. 286

CLEANER, mornings. — Apply Manager, Roman Candle, Hanley. x 285

CLEANERS 2 required. — Apply: Manager, Normacot Hotel, Longton. Phone 33569. 284

CLEANERS required, female, Silverdale area, 9 a.m.-12 noon. — Phone S.O.T. 87740. 284

CLEANER required 6 mornings, 2½ hours, child not objected to. — Plume of Feathers, Barlaston, 2478. 284

CLERK, male or female for Wages, Costing and Ledger, Electrical Engineers Office. — Barnett Soans, South Wolfe-st., Stoke. Phone 44489. 284

COMMERCIAL Vehicle Fitter required, good rates of pay for experienced man, capable of working on own initiative, good opportunities for overtime. — Tel. S.O.T. 262296. 285

COMMIS Chef for busy kitchen, servicing restaurant, cafeteria and outside catering, 4½-day week. — Phone: Newcastle 619013 after 7 p.m. 285

COOK / Manageress required for new Remploy Factory, at London-rd., Newcastle, to open shortly, must be experienced in all aspects of cooking, costing and buying, 5 day week, excellent conds., 17 days holiday, good salary. — Apply: The Manager, Barracks-rd., Newcastle. Phone 615053. 285

CRESSWELL'S, Longton, require male Counter Assistant, good rates of pay 5 day week, Saturday working. — Tel. 33488/35121. 284

Situations Vacant

A 1 Copy the sentences and fill in the blanks from the words in brackets:

If you look in the_____ _____part of your local paper, you may be able to find a_____ (job, vacant, situations).

2 How many advertisements are there for bar-staff and barmaids? How many are there for cleaners?

3 Look through the 'cleaners' section. What sort of work would a cleaner have to do at the *Roman Candle* or the *Plume of Feathers*?

4 Write down the correct reply:

Hanley, Newcastle, Longton and Biddulph are
a) pubs, b) towns, c) counties.

5 What number would you telephone if you were interested in a job as
a ladies' hairdresser
a petrol-pump attendant
a shop assistant?

6 You are twenty years old. You are bored with your present job. Your hobby is painting. You know a lot about it. Which job may interest you?

7 You are sixteen years old. You'd like to be a typist. You have done well in typing lessons at school. You see a post which appeals to you, and you want to apply for the job. Who do you write to?

8 Find the meanings of these words and phrases:
**applicant   personnel officer
previous experience required
transport provided   salary   vacant.**

B 1 Write out a letter of application for one of the jobs in the Situations Vacant columns. Give your age, your best school subjects and your reasons for applying.

2 Find out which are the five jobs most often referred to in the Situations Vacant section of your local paper for one week. Write them down.

'I'm not sure you'd do for this sort of work, sir.'

27

Entertainment

Entertainment

Today's Cinemas

A 1 In which cinema would I be able to see:
 The Odessa File; The Amazons; Clones?
 2 Omar Sharif is my favourite actor. Where can I go to
 see him? Which film is he appearing in?
 3 Which film could I see at 7.20 pm? Which film could
 I see at 3.25 pm?

Theatres

4 Copy and complete this table:

Theatre	Play	Time of Showing

Olympic Variety Club

5 Write down only the **true** sentences:
 The telephone number of the Olympic Variety
 Club is SOT 533590.
 On Friday and Saturday you can see Joe Dolan
 and the Drifters.
 On Wednesday, November 27th, you can see the
 Barrie Brothers.
 Tickets for Wednesday, November 27th, are
 available for £1 each.
 There is no car park.

Dancing and Entertainment

6 What opens on November 23rd?
 What is a discotheque?
 What is the entrance price to the discotheque?
 What do you think the **cockloft** is?

B 1 It is Saturday night. You have £5 to spend. Look at
 the clips on the opposite page and write down where
 you will go and how you will spend your money.
 Don't forget you will need some money for the bus
 or taxi. Compare your answer with your friend's.
 2 How were people entertained before cinemas, clubs
 and discos? Find out about the music-hall and write
 a few lines on it. Your history teacher may help you.

29

Births and Marriages

Coming of Age

WHITEHOUSE (Ann). — Congratulations, best wishes on your 21st birthday. Lots of love. — Mum, Dad, Nell.
z 290

Engagements

KENT — FREARSON. — The engagement is announced between Anthony, son of Mr. and Mrs. D. W. Kent, of Baddeley Edge and Denise, daughter of Mr. and Mrs. J. W. Frearson, of Hanley. — Congratulations both families.
y 290

SHERRATT—MARSH. — Congratulations Steve and Jan. on your engagement. — Love. — From both families.
z 290

Forthcoming Marriage

PHILIPS — HEWITT. — Mr. and Mrs. S. Hewitt, of 78, Wimbourne-ave., Blurton, are pleased to announce the marriage of their daughter Carole Anne, to Terry, son of Mr. and Mrs H. Phillips, of 84, Barlaston-rd., Blurton, at Blurton Parish Church, on Saturday, Dec. 7th. — Congratulations to both.
290

Marriages

SMITH—COOK—On Nov. 27th, Gill, daughter of Mrs. and the late Mr. H. E. Cook, of Barlaston, to Peter, son of Mr. and Mrs. D. Smith, of Trentham.
b 290

Wedding Anniversaries
GOLDEN WEDDINGS

MAHON. — Congratulations Mum and Dad on your Golden Wedding. — All our love Jean, Arthur, Diane.
290

SKINNER — Mr. and Mrs. Richard Skinner (nee Lily Payne) present address, 1, Blackelow-rd., Abbey Hulton. — Congratulations Mum and Dad on your golden wedding anniversary. — With love from all your family. God bless you both.
290

Births

LONGMORE (nee Cooke). — To Glenys and Harold, a precious gift of a Daughter (Kerry Ann), a sister for Ian, born Nov. 15th. H.M.H. — Thanking staff, friends, neighbours.
b 278

LONGMORE. — Congratulations Glenis and Harold and welcome to Ian's beautiful little sister (Kerry Anne). All our love. — Mavis, Brian and children.
b 278

MOORE (nee Aston). — To Chris and Dave, on Nov. 18th, a Brother (Ian Thomas) for Louise. — Thanks to the staff at Congleton War Memorial Hospital.
b 279

SIMS (nee Rutter). — Sheila and David are pleased to announce the safe arrival of Natalie Jane, on Nov. 9th, 1974. — Thanking staff at N.S.M.H.

Birthday Greetings

HASSALL (Edna). — All our love and best wishes on your 60th birthday. — From Albert, Geoffrey, Eileen, Billy, Julie, John.
b 286

LAWTON (Ethel). — 14, Ryder-rd., Meir. To mother with all our ever-lasting love on your 80th birthday. Health and happiness always. — From Mona and Ray, Ray, Brenda and Russell.
b 286

LAWTON (Ethel). — To mother with all our love on your 80th birthday. Wishing you all the best in life. — From Ethel, Jack, John, Sylvia, Ray, Sharon and Mark.
b 286

BAGNALL (Jon). — Congratulations son on your 21st Birthday. Love. — Mam, Dad, Brothers and Sister.
b 286

Births and Marriages

A 1 What do these terms mean?

   Coming of Age   Forthcoming Marriage
   Golden Wedding   Wedding Anniversaries

2 Copy down these names, and by the side of each
   name write the section it belongs to (births,
   engagements, etc.):

   Sherratt-Marsh; Skinner; Hassall; Sims;
   Whitehouse.

3 In the Births section, what is the name of Glenis
   and Harold Longmore's newly-born daughter?

4 How old is Mrs Ethel Lawton?
   Who is 60?

5 What are the engaged couple's christian names in
   the Kent-Frearson entry?

6 Where do Mr and Mrs Phillips live?

7 Look at the Births section. Find the word **née.**
   Ask your teacher what it means.

8 Look at the Births section again. What do you think
   the letters MH mean in HMH and NSMH?

9 Why are there two names for each entry in the
   Engagements section?

10 Look at Bagnall (Birthday Greetings). This entry
   might have been put in another section. Which one?

11 What other headings can you think of besides
   Births, Marriages, etc?

12 Who congratulates mum and dad Mahon on their
   Golden Wedding Anniversary?

B 1 How long do you think you should be engaged before
   you marry?

2 What do you think is the best age for getting
   married?

3 What sort of person would you like your wife or
   husband to be?

4 Why is it important that you get on well with your
   in-laws?

'I've heard of worried fathers, but ...'

Just Married

Her own bridal creation

A LOT of patient work went into the making of the wedding dress worn by Christine Elma Cuthbertson at her wedding today.

For the dress, a full-length white crepe gown, with an embroidered panel inset was made by the bride.

Christine, an expert needle-woman who makes all her own clothes, worked flower-heads on the inset against a background of velvet ribbon lattice. She also made her headdress — and decorated it with embroidered flowers.

Secretary to the General Manager of the Evening Sentinel, Mr. M. A. Hallas, Christine is the daughter of Mr. and Mrs. A. J. Cuthbertson, of 7, Jesmond-grove, Blurton.

The bridegroom, Mr. Ian James Hudson, a salesman with a local bakery, is the son of Mr. and Mrs. C. H. Hudson, of 4, Consett-road, Blurton.

The wedding took place at St. Bartholomew's Church, Blurton, and the Rev. A. E. Farley officiated.

The only bridesmaid was Miss Margaret Cuthbertson, the bride's sister, and best man was Mr. Geoffrey Harrison.

Just Married

A 1 Copy out and complete the sentences by choosing
the correct word or phrase from those in brackets:
   The bride's name is_____
   (Ann Cuthbertson, Elma Bertson, Christine
   Elma Cuthbertson).
   The dress is a full-length white gown made from
   _____ (silk, crepe, satin, lace).
   Christine makes_____ (her own clothes,
   rabbit hutches, crepe flowers).
   The bride is the daughter of_____ (Mr and
   Mrs Hallas, Mr and Mrs A. J. Cuthbertson).
   The bridegroom's name is_____ (Ian, Fred,
   William, John, James, Sydney).
   He is a_____ (baker, dressmaker,
   salesman, cake-maker).
   The Reverend A. E. Farley was the_____
   (best man, vicar, bridesmaid, groom, bride).
   There was_____ bridesmaid. (one, two,
   three, four, five)
   Mr G. Harrison was_____ (the vicar, a good
   man, the best man, a baker).

B 1 What is **a groom** **a best man**
   a bridesmaid?
   2 Write a description of the bride opposite.
   3 Draw either a wedding dress or an outfit for the
   groom.
   4 What would you like to wear if you get married?
   Write a few lines down.

33

'UPSET' MAN KICKED IN DOORS

ANNOYED by two men who stared at him, 26-years-old Peter Alan Slater left the Top of the World ballroom, Stafford, and kicked in two shop doors, Stafford Magistrates were told yesterday.

Sergeant Eric Simpson, prosecuting, said Slater first of all kicked at a glass panel in the front door of Sportsco, Ltd., then ran off and did the same to a door in the new Stafford shopping precinct.

When seen by police, Slater, said: "I got upset at the Top of the World when two men kept annoying me. I was thinking of them at the time and I just kicked the window."

Slater of Sandon-road, Stafford, admitted two offences of committing criminal damage to glass panelled doors total value £37.18 and the case was adjourned until January 2nd for reports. He was allowed bail.

'Wanton damage' by boys

TWO FIFTEEN - YEARS - OLD boys caused "sheer wanton damage" to machinery on a Tunstall building site, Mr. Tom Bradburn, prosecuting, told the City Juvenile Court at Fenton today.

They smashed the glass on a cement mixer dialling unit and ripped away the dials, then they found a water pump and filled it with sand and rubbish off the building site.

That escapade caused damage worth £200, but the story did not finish there, Mr Bradburn said, for the boys then went to Tunstall park where they smashed 16 panes of glass behind the bandstand. This cost another £14.

Compensation

They were both placed under supervision for 12 months and ordered to pay £7 compensation each towards the broken windows.

Clothes stolen in raid on boutique

Girls' trendy clothes worth about £1,000 have been stolen in a raid on a Leek boutique.

Taken from the Girl Boutique, in Brook-street, were at least 40 pairs of trousers, 36 blouses, 26 skirts, 29 dresses, 55 sweaters, 5 jackets 15 long skirts, as well as trousers suits, jumpers, and evening tops, representing about three quarters of the stock.

The theft is believed to have occurred between Wednesday night and this morning, when the discovery was made by the proprietor. Most of the racks were cleared

Offences

Upset Man Kicked in Doors

A 1 These sentences have been taken from the clip but they are jumbled up. See if you can write them down properly, giving each a capital letter and a full stop:

 in two kicked Slater doors shop

 men annoying me said two kept Slater

 was bail allowed he

2 These words are taken from the clip but they are not complete. Fill in the blanks. Each blank is one letter.

 Mag _ _ _ r _ _ _   _ rec _ _ _ _

 a _ m _ _ _ _ d   _ _ _ min _ _

  _ dj _ _ _ ned

Now find out what the words mean.

3 Who was prosecuting?

How much were the doors worth?

Wanton Damage by Boys

4 Look at the clip for the answers to these questions:

Write down the sentence with the word **escapade** in it.

Write down the two things that the boys did.

Where was the machinery?

5 What does **supervision** mean? What is **compensation**?

Clothes Stolen in Raid on Boutique

6 Which word in the first part of the article means the opposite of out of date?

7 Make a list of the items stolen. Use a separate line for each item.

B Write a newspaper report (about half a page) on the theft of some cakes from a bakery, *or* on two girls being found after they had run away from home.

Local Sport

Selection poser for Port Vale Manager

PORT VALE Manager Roy Sproson faces the tough decision of either fielding an unchanged team against Bury at home on Saturday or finding room for Ray Williams.

Williams has missed Vale's last three games with a back injury but has now passed himself fit to present Mr. Sproson with a problem.

Deputy for Williams at Peterborough was Keith Chadwick, who scored a goal in Vale's fine 2-0 win last Saturday and played well.

Says Mr. Sproson: "It would be hard on Keith to find himself left out after that performance at Peterborough but, of course, we cannot afford to overlook Ray's claims. His form this season has been superb."

JUNIOR CRICKET ON SUNDAYS

Sunday cricket gets under way in the Kidsgrove and District Junior League next season, with eight clubs taking part.

The clubs are: Audley, Burslem, Caverswall, Cheadle, Crewe Rolls-Royce, Great Chell, Leek and Sneyd.

The decision will give youngsters experience of five-hour matches, instead of the present three hours played in mid-week.

The experiment will be watched with interest by the other clubs forming the Western and Eastern Sections.

Scot Hay were elected back into the league after assuring members that they already had around 19 young players wishing to take part. They will play in the Western Section.

Silverdale, Ashcombe Park and Sandyford, bottom clubs in the three sections this year, were re-elected.

League Treasurer Mr. E. Farley warned that they were only just breaking even financially, but as the figures had not been circulated it was decided to debate the issues at a later meeting.

Mr. H. S. Trafford was elected President and Committee Chairman for the sixth year, but hinted that he felt it would be wrong to stay in the position for too long, suggesting that the two posts might be split up in the future.

Other officers appointed:— Secretary, Mr. R. Cherry; Treasurer, Mr. E. Farley; Assistant Secretary, Mr. H. Unett; Vice-Chairman, Mr. W. S. Hutchinson.

Mr. D. Hall, of Sneyd, was added to the list of Vice-Presidents.

36

Local Sport

Selection Poser for Port Vale Manager

A 1 Who faces what in the first paragraph?
  2 Why hadn't Williams been playing in Vale's last three games?
  3 Who was Williams's stand-in at Peterborough?
  4 Why is Roy Sproson's decision difficult to make?
  5 What does 'fielding an unchanged team' mean?

Junior Cricket on Sundays

  6 Answer **yes** or **no**:
    Are seven clubs taking part in the Kidsgrove and District Junior league?
    Is Crewe Rolls-Royce one of the teams?
  7 Choose the right answer from the pair of answers and write it down:
    { Scot Hay had 91 players wishing to take part.
    { Scot Hay will play in the Western Section.

    { Silverdale was not re-elected.
    { Sandyford was re-elected together with Silverdale and Ashcombe Park.

  8 Who was Mr H. S. Trafford, and what did he hint?
  9 Here is one officer, and his position:
    Mr R. Cherry – Secretary
  Now write down the names and positions of the other officers.

B 1 Copy out from your local paper any brief sports reports which interest you.

  2 Find out what the word **bias** means. Are any of the sports reports you've read biased in favour of (or against) a particular team, do you think?

'Enjoy the game last Saturday?'

37

For Sale / Wanted

Private Bargains £10 and under

AIR Rifle, B.S.A. Meteor 022, £8. — Phone Churnet Side 360320. 288

APOLLO 2-Piece Cue, as new, £4. — 16, Castlehill-rd., Newcastle. b 288

AS new Toy Casdon Cooker, Sink Unit, Washer, £2.50 each; Spanish Guitar £1.50. — 60, Park-rd., Silverdale. 288

ATTRACTIVE Long Dress, navy / white, lace top, 18s, £8, 2 Tops £2. — Tel. 564144. 288

BABY'S Playpen, with wooden floor, ideal for Christmas, £3. — Blythe Bridge 4789. b 288

BABY Pram, red, converts to pushchair and carrycot, £10. — Ring Newcastle 621480. 288

BABYDAYS Pushchair by Raleigh, navy, canvas body, hood and cover, very good condition, £10. — Wetley Rocks 550757. 288

BARGAIN: Two 550 x 12 Tyres, suitable 1300. — Tel. 318011, after 3.0 p.m. 289

BARGAIN: Smart Brown Warm Trouser Suit, worn only twice, £7, 14s/16s. — Tel. 564144. 288

BICYCLE with stabilisers, £5; Board and Easel, £2; Lady's Crash Helmet, £3. — Tel. 503072. 288

BIKE with stabilisers, exc. cond., suit age 3 to 6, £8. — 8, Longbrook-ave., Blurton, S.O.T. d 288

BLACK Patchwork Long Waistcoat, size 14/16, as new, £5. — Phone Newcastle 562107. 288

BOY'S Sports Bike, 18in. frame, 3-speed, £10. — 216, Trent Valley-rd., Oakhill. 288

BOY'S Raleigh Cycle, suit age 7-9 years, £8. — 37, Wattlands-ave., Wolstanton. 288

CANTILEVER Tool Box and Tools, £10. — 410, Beverley-drive, Bentilee; after 6 p.m.

CARRYCOT and Stand, Playpen and Baby Walker, £10 the lot. — Tel.

Private Bargains £10 and under

FOR Sale, 3 Tyres, size 400 x 8 with wheels, 2 Michelin as new, £8. — Tel 659434. z 288

FOR Sale, New World 84 Gas Cooker, good cond., £10 o.n.o. — Tel. 617491. b 288

FOR Sale: Electric Cooker, good condition, £6. — Apply between 6 p.m.- 8 p.m.: 27, Harcourt-st., Shelton. 288

FOR Sale: Small Accordian, suit child, exc. cond., £10 o.n.o. — Apply: 148, Broadway, Meir. b 288

FOR Sale: Modern Birdcage and Stand, in very good condition, and 2 Budgies, £7. — Tel. Cheadle 3008 after 6 p.m. 288

FOUR Volumes of World of the Children, as new, £5. — Barlaston 2805. 288

FOUR Morris 1000 Wheels, with good tyres, one new, £6. — Tel. 84803. 288

FRIDGE for sale, good working order, £10. — Apply: 1, Trentham-grove, May Bank. 288

GAS Cooker for sale, exc. condition, £10. — 117, Bath-rd., Silverdale. 288

GRUNDIG TK400 Tape Recorder, £10. — Tel. 318580. 288

GUITAR with plastic bag, not quite full-size, £8. — Tel. Blythe Bridge 4083. 288

GUITAR, £3.50; Child's Workbench, £1.50. — Shaw, 55, Haymer-grove, Weston Coyney (off Caverswall-rd.). 288

GUITAR Steel Strings, as new, excellent condition, cost £9, accept £6. — Tel. 619419. 288

HIGH Dome Pressure Cooker, £5. — Ring 85974, after 5.30 p.m. 288

INTERIOR Door, as new, £3. — Apply after 6 p.m., 62, Long Valley-rd., Gillow Heath, Biddulph. y 288

LADY'S Leather Platform Boots, black, size 4, exc. cond., £4. — Tel. 317855.

Miscellaneous Wants

DIMPLEX Radiator, small or bathroom type. — Phone Barlaston 2897. y 284

WANTED: Twintub Washer up to £15. — Stevenson, Burslem 86483. 284

WANTED: Garden Shed. — Phone S.O.T. 317161. 284

WANTED: Violin, good cond. — Phone 49743, after 5.30. d 285

WANTED: Chipper Style Cycle, to suit boy 6 years old. — Leek 6118. 284

FISHING Gear wanted. — Phone 46557. d 284

QUALITY Portable Typewriter, cash for good example. — Stone 4649. 284

CLARINET wanted. — Tel. Alsager 2423. 284

ELECTRIC Sewing Machine. — Ring Rudyard £10. 284

WANTED: Petite Typewriter, exc. cond. — Tel. 614827. 284

KL Jeenay Child's Seat and Junior Safety Harness wanted. — 617616. 284

JUMBLE Sales cleared. — Plant, Dilhorne, S.O.T. 550413. f 284

WANTED: Single Wardrobe. — Tel. 263686 after 5 p.m. x 284

WANTED: Electric Train Set with Accessories. — Phone 311619. 285

WANTED Old Chip Shop hand Potato Chipper. — Ring Cheadle 2126. 284

LOG / coal effect Gas Fire. — Kidsgrove 5857. 284

TEAK Fitted 3ft. Wardrobe or Combination. — Tel. 533446. 284

CHILD'S Desk and Chair, good cond. — Phone Blythe Bridge 9326. 284

WANTED: Scalextric with transformer. — Ring 310112. 284

WANTED: 5ft. Billiard Table. — Phone 25637. y 284

BICYCLE suitable for boy 12 to 14 years. — Tel. Stone 3504. 284

WEIGHT Lifting Tackle, up to 100th. weights. — Tel. 617081. 284

SCRAP collected—Top prices paid. Tel: Hankey Abbey Hulton 541374. 283

WANTED: Portable Typewriter, good cond. — Tel. 622763. 284

For Sale / Wanted

For Sale

A 1 Where would I go to if I wanted to buy a second-hand tool box? OXFAMS
   Where would I go to if I wanted to buy a bike with a three-speed gear?
   Where could I get an accordian from?
   2 Which telephone number would I ring for a) an air rifle; b) a lady's crash helmet; c) a Grundig tape recorder?
   3 How much would I have to pay for a) a fridge; b) an interior door?
   4 What could I buy from
      a) 55 Hayner Grove, Western Coyney;
      b) 27 Harcourt St, Shelton?
   5 I ring 564144. What do I want?

Miscellaneous Wants

   6 What does **miscellaneous** mean?
   7 You have the following items for sale. Write down the ones you can sell through the Miscellaneous Wants column:
      a train set; a typewriter; a sewing machine; a tool chest; an electric kettle; a violin; a billiard table.
   8 I ring Cheadle 2126. What do I have to sell?

B 1 You want to sell an article for £8. Write out an advertisement, stating what the article is, and your address or telephone number.
   2 You want to buy a second-hand bicycle. Write out an advertisement to put in the Miscellaneous Wants column. Give details of the sort of bike you'd like, and your telephone number. If you don't have a telephone, make a number up.
   3 Look at the For Sale columns of your local paper. Pick out ten articles which are being sold second-hand. Find out how much each would cost new. Find out how much you would save in each case by buying the article second-hand.

Useful Ideas

What's Cooking?
by Sylvia Frost

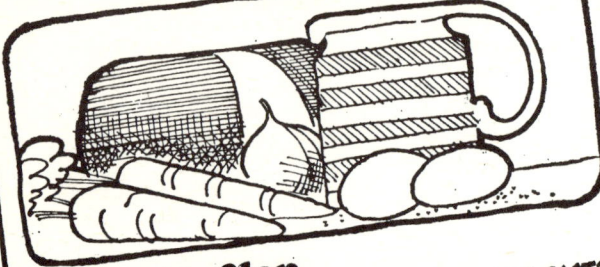

Vegetable flan

LINE AN 8" FLAN CASE WITH SHORTCRUST PASTRY. PEEL AND CHOP 1 MEDIUM-SIZED ONION AND 3 CARROTS. SLICE 4oz MUSHROOMS.

HEAT 1oz BUTTER AND TOSS THE VEGETABLES IN THIS FOR A FEW MINUTES. ALLOW THE VEGETABLES TO COOL AND PUT THEM INTO THE PASTRY CASE.

BEAT 2 EGGS, ADD ¼ PT MILK, 4oz GRATED GOUDA CHEESE, SALT AND PEPPER. THEN POUR THE MIXTURE OVER THE VEGETABLES.

BAKE IN A MODERATE OVEN (375-400°F, GAS MARKS 5-6) FOR 25-30 MINUTES UNTIL THE PASTRY BEGINS TO BROWN.

LOWER THE HEAT AND COOK FOR A FURTHER 15 MINUTES UNTIL THE CHEESE FILLING IS SET. SERVE HOT OR COLD WITH SALAD.

(SERVES 4)

7. © Advance Features

Tip Top Tip

NECK NEXT

Put that excess hand cream to good use! When you find you've got too much on your hands, wipe them over your neck — too often a neglected area.

Tip Top Tips

PRETTY PRACTICAL!

Next time you're making a long cotton skirt, get sufficient extra material to make a long cotton pinny to go with it. Pretty **and** practical!

40

Useful Ideas

What's Cooking?

A 1 What does the word **ingredient** mean?
  2 Here is a list of the ingredients of the Vegetable Flan, and another list of the amounts needed. Rewrite the list, putting the right amount against each ingredient:

onion	¼ pint
mushrooms	2
gouda cheese	1 oz
carrots	4 oz
eggs	4 oz
milk	1
butter	3

  3 How long is the flan baked for altogether?

Tip Top Tips

  4 Copy out the two tips.
  5 Which tip is the more useful of the two? Why, do you think?

6 Write down the word from the 'Neck Next' tip which means 'not paid enough attention to'. Write down the word from 'Pretty Practical' which means 'enough'. Which word means 'too much'?

B 1 If you know a useful tip, write it down.
  2 Copy down a simple recipe you have used either at home or in school.
  3 Can you think of anything useful that can be made from things people usually throw away? (E.g. some people have made models from matchsticks.) Write down one or two suggestions.

Local Council Issues

Council seek assurance on Sunday trading

AN ASSURANCE that there will be strict observance of conditions banning Sunday trading when a new do-it-yourself centre is opened in Willaston village, was sought by the Parish Council last night.

The council were considering detailed plans to convert a timber yard in Coppice-road, into a centre for the sale of do-it-yourself materials and ironmongery.

Mr. Cyril Peake said that residents should be entitled to at least one day's peace and quiet in the week.

It was agreed to ask Crewe and Nantwich Borough Council's Development Committee who are to consider the application to bear in mind the conditions imposed by the old rural council.

THEY SAY: 'KNOCK IT DOWN'

TYRLEY Parish Council are to urge again that Peatswood Hall be demolished and a replacement building erected on the site.

At their meeting last night, members expressed their concern that Newcastle Borough Council had refused permission for the owner, Mr. Roger Hewitt, to replace the existing property with a new building.

Peatswood Hall is a listed building and has architectural and historic interest.

Colonel John Congreave said that the building was "riddled with dry rot" and believed that about £200,000 would have to be spent to preserve it.

"It will not be of much historic interest when it has fallen down—which is what will happen if it is left," he said.

Mr. George Butter said that the borough council should be pressed to change their decision about the hall and it was agreed that the parish council write to them.

Local Council Issues

Council Seek Assurance on Sunday Trading

A 1 On the left are five words from the clip, and on the right five meanings. See if you can match each word with its correct meaning.

assurance	people living in a place
observance	belonging to the countryside
convert	a promise
residents	taking notice of
rural	to change into something else

2 What is sought by the Parish Council?
Who should be entitled to at least one day's peace and quiet?
3 What do you think the Parish Council are most worried about?

They Say Knock It Down

4 Which sentence out of each pair of sentences is correct?
{ Tyrley Parish Council says knock down Peatswood Hall.
Tyrley Parish Council says repair Peatswood Hall.

{ Colonel Congreave said Peatswood Hall was in excellent condition.
Colonel Congreave said Peatswood Hall was 'riddled with dry rot'.

{ Mr Roger Hewitt wanted to replace the hall with a new building.
Mr Roger Hewitt wanted to keep the old hall.

5 Find out what 'architectural and historic interest' means.

B 1 Read this: 'Peatswood Hall is a listed building and has architectural and historic interest.'
Find out what a listed building is.
2 Write down the names of any listed buildings in your area. Find out if any of them are due to be demolished, and why. Your teacher will help you.

Local Events

Santa Claus arrives at Newcastle

Father Christmas, complete with his entourage of fairies and a bunny, arrived at Newcastle on Saturday — in good cheer, despite the rain.

Hundreds of cheering children welcomed Santa outside the Debenhams store in the town centre as he rolled up in a black Rolls-Royce.

Inside the store, he again greeted children in the specially prepared grotto, helped along by store girls Denise Kent, aged 17, dressed as a fairy, Sylvia Shuttlebotham, 18, Delia Brown, 20, Janet Hambleton, 19, 17-years-old Julie Leese and "bunny" Denise Colley, aged 16.

Santa Claus will be at the store every Saturday until Christmas.

SOLOISTS SHINE IN TUNEFUL 'NABUCCO'

THE COMBINATION of the City of Stoke-on-Trent Choral Society, the Manchester Mozart Symphony Orchestra and some fine vocal performances produced a stimulating interpretation of the concert arrangement of Verdi's Grand Opera "Nabucco" last night.

The work, Verdi's first "hit," found an appreciative response in Hanley Town Hall, particularly for baritone Malcolm Rivers in the title role and soprano Janice Chapman as Abigail — two of the five soloists who between them handled eight characterisations.

The opera, both dramatic and tuneful, provided plenty of scope for the chorus whose real moment of glory came in act three with the famous moving song, "On the Banks of the Euphrates."

The range and quality of Miss Chapman's voice was best demonstrated in the Scene and Air in act two and fellow soprano Joyce Stringer's finest moment came near the end with the Funeral March and Prayer.

Noel Noble, bass, also made some notable contributions, particularly the Prayer in act two, accompanied by six cellos of the orchestra, under the baton of John Padmore.

Perhaps the most moving episode in the concert was the duet between Malcolm Rivers and Janice Chapman in act three, an appealing piece deeply ingrained with pathos. The other soloist was tenor Edward Byles.

Local Events

Santa Claus Arrives at Newcastle

A 1 Copy out these sentences and add one word so that
they make sense.

Father Christmas arrived at_____ .

_____ of children welcomed Santa.

Santa pulled up outside the_____ store in
the town centre.

2 Write down the names of the store girls who helped
Santa Claus.

Write them down so that their surnames come in
alphabetical order.

Write the age of each girl by her name.

3 This cutting was taken from a newspaper dated
Monday, November 11th, 1974. It tells us that Santa
arrived the Saturday before – November 9th.

How many visits altogether will he have made to the
store before Christmas?

Soloists Shine in Tuneful Nabucco

4 Find out the meanings of these words and phrases.
Your teacher will help you:

stimulating interpretation   opera
concert arrangement   under the baton of
ingrained with pathos   soloist.

5 What is said about the following performers:
Malcolm Rivers, Janice Chapman, Joyce Stringer,
Noel Noble, John Padmore, Edward Byles?

6 What sort of music would you say is described in the
clip? Is it pop music, light music, serious music?
Which one?

7 What is the opera called? What famous song comes
in act three?

B 1 You have brought your little sister to Newcastle to
see Santa. Write a description of his arrival at the
store.

2 Find out all you can about the Italian composer,
Verdi.

3 Ask your music teacher to explain **soprano,
baritone, tenor** and **bass.**

Records of singers could help you here.

Tame bird 'rules roost'

PETS

CON GORDON

A READER has a blackbird who enters the house and makes himself at home in the kitchen.

"He enters at the back door and makes a whimpering noise," she writes. "That means 'I'm here.'

"If you pay no heed he penetrates deeper and utters a harsher note which means 'You're not taking any notice of me.'

"If you still disregard him he parades about the kitchen making a persistent, belling noise which means 'Aren't you going to give me something?'

"He loves cheese and insists on having it fresh and crumbly. If it is hard and stale he throws it back at you.

"If he can't get in at the back door there's a pantomime at the kitchen window. He parades up and down the outside window-sill and whistles and squawks.

"When we talk and whistle to him he chatters and whistles back. When there's a cat about he carries on alarming, bobbing his head in its direction and turning to us as much as to say, 'Can't you see what's down the garden?'

"He comes seven days a week except when we're on holiday. I often wonder what he does in our absence but he's always back when we are. Usually he calls for breakfast and then at intervals during the day.

"The sparrows are his chief enemy. He won't let them drink from his bath and if they follow him in a mob he picks up his cheese and flies off with it, chuntering.

"We have had friendly thrushes and blackbirds before but Blackie is by far the most intelligent. He walked in after crumbs three years ago and has been with us ever since.

"He would be all over the house if we let him. He thinks he owns the place."

Pets

A 1 Find out what these words from the clip mean:
penetrates   persistent   parades chuntering.

2 Answer **true** or **not true**:

When the blackbird makes a whimpering noise it means that he has arrived.

If no attention is paid to the blackbird he flies off.

The blackbird loves bread and milk.

If the blackbird can't get in through the door, he flies down the chimney.

3 Answer **yes** or **no**:

When the cat is about, does the blackbird fly over to it?

Does the blackbird come seven days a week?

Is his name Blackie?

Is he frightened of people?

4 Fill in the blanks with words from the article:

Blackie is an＿＿＿＿ bird. Blackie thinks he ＿＿＿＿ ＿＿＿＿place. He likes his cheese to be＿＿＿＿and＿＿＿＿ .

B 1 Write about half a page on a pet. It could be your own pet, or one belonging to your friend.

2 Read any animal articles you can find in your paper.

3 How would you look after a young bird that had fallen from its nest and been left by its parents?

4 How do you think early men trained wild dogs to hunt with them?

'It's for you.'

Contents